SEPAR*ATIONS*

DIVORCE

by Janine Amos
Illustrated by Gwen Green
Photographs by Angela Hampton

Gareth Stevens Publishing
A WORLD ALMANAC EDUCATION GROUP COMPANY

Please visit our web site at: www.garethstevens.com
For a free color catalog describing Gareth Stevens Publishing's list of high-quality books and multimedia programs, call 1-800-542-2595 or fax your request to (414) 332-3567.

Library of Congress Cataloging-in-Publication Data

Amos, Janine.
    Divorce / text by Janine Amos; illustrations by Gwen Green; photography by
Angela Hampton.
       p. cm. — (Separations)
    Includes bibliographical references.
    Summary: Uses letters, stories, and informational text to provide advice for children
on how to cope with their parents' divorce.
    ISBN 0-8368-3090-3 (lib. bdg.)
    1. Divorce—Juvenile literature. 2. Children of divorced parents—Juvenile literature.
[1. Divorce.] I. Green, Gwen, ill. II. Hampton, Angela, ill. III. Title.
HQ814.A53   2002
306.89—dc21   2001054954

This edition first published in 2002 by
Gareth Stevens Publishing
A World Almanac Education Group Company
330 West Olive Street, Suite 100
Milwaukee, WI 53212 USA

This U.S. edition © 2002 by Gareth Stevens, Inc. First published in 1997 by Cherrytree Press, a subsidiary of Evans Brothers Limited. © 1997 by Cherrytree (a member of the Evans Group of Publishers), 2A Portman Mansions, Chiltern Street, London W1M 1LE, United Kingdom. This U.S. edition published under license from Evans Brothers Limited. Additional end matter © 2002 by Gareth Stevens, Inc.

Gareth Stevens cover design and page layout: Tammy Gruenewald
Gareth Stevens series editor: Dorothy L. Gibbs

Printed in the United States of America

1 2 3 4 5 6 7 8 9 06 05 04 03 02

Contents

Letters: Dear Grandma — Dear Tom   4

Story: Christmas Spirit   6

Letters: Dear Sally — Dear Donna   12

Feelings: It's Hard for Everyone   14

How to Help Yourself Cope   16

Letters: Dear Grandma — Dear Tom   18

Feelings: Better or Worse?   20

Getting On with Your New Life   22

Story: Locked Out   24

Letters: Dear Sally — Dear Donna   30

More Books to Read — Web Sites   32

Dear Grandma,
Thank you for my birthday money. I'm buying a new game for my computer.
Last night Dad told me he was leaving. He doesn't like living here anymore so he's going to live in an apartment by himself.
Dad says he'll see me on the weekends and I can stay at his apartment some school days too. The same thing happened to Jack, but his dad's always going away now and he doesn't see him very much. He gives him kids' toys for his birthday like he doesn't know how old he is. I wish things could go back to how they were. Mom's crying all the time and shouting. It's horrible.
Are you coming to see us?
love Tom

Dear Tom,

I'm glad you wrote to me. It's a hard time for you all, and you must be feeling very upset and confused.

Sometimes grown-ups can't get along anymore. They stop loving each other, but they don't stop loving you. Your mom and dad both love you very much, and both of them want to be with you. Remember that.

I'm sorry that your friend Jack doesn't see his father very often. That doesn't mean the same thing will happen to you. If your dad says he'll see you every week, then that's what he plans to do.

Your mom and dad are very hurt and sad at the moment, Tom. Keep talking to them. Tell them how you feel. You can always talk to me, either in a letter or on the telephone.

I'm thinking of you, and I'm coming to see you soon.

With love,
Grandma

Christmas Spirit

Bang! bang! bang! went Danny's foot against the kitchen chair. He knew it annoyed his mom, but, today, she pretended not to notice. Instead, she turned on the radio, and a Christmas carol blared out. Danny hated the sound. He hated the Christmassy smells coming from his mom's cooking, too. Danny hated most things since his dad moved out.

Danny's mom handed him some knives and forks.

"Hurry up and set the table, Danny," she said. "Grandma and Grandpa will be here soon."

Danny's mom smiled, but her eyes looked sad.

"It doesn't feel like Christmas without Dad," thought Danny. "Why is Mom trying to pretend everything's the same?"

Danny scowled. He had wanted to say this to his mom, but she always got upset when he talked about Dad.

"You'll feel better when Grandma and Grandpa get here," said his mom gently.

"No, I won't!" shouted Danny. "It will be worse — much worse!"

Danny threw down the knives and forks and rushed out of the room.

In his bedroom, Danny reached for Fred Bear. His old, battered teddy bear wasn't really a baby toy, Danny told himself. Fred was more like a mascot. Whatever Fred was, Danny needed him badly right now.

"It's not that I don't want to see Grandma and Grandpa," Danny explained to the bear, "but they always come for Christmas dinner. Doing everything the same will make me miss Dad more."

Just then, the doorbell rang.

"Let's go!" whispered Danny.

With Fred tucked safely in his jacket, Danny tiptoed down the hall, crept downstairs, and sneaked out the back door.

Outside, there was a small shed. It was full of
camping gear and old motorcycle magazines.
Mom and Danny called it "Dad's Place."
Danny slipped inside and cleared
off a place to sit down. It
was cold and dark
in the shed.

Soon, Danny's tummy rumbled. He felt in his pockets and pulled out
some lint-covered chocolate. It was a piece left over from the candy bar
his dad had given him last Saturday. Danny slowly began to munch. He
wondered if his dad was eating Christmas dinner by himself. Two tears
rolled down Danny's cheeks.

Bright light streamed into the shed when Danny's mom opened the door. Danny waited to be sent back into the house. Instead, his mom came in and sat down next to him. She gave him a hug.

"Dad's never coming back home to live, is he?" whispered Danny.

"No," replied his mom quietly.

"Christmas makes it even harder," sighed Danny. "I wish we were a real family."

Danny's mom thought for a while. "We're a different kind of family now," she said at last, "and some things we do will be a little different. Today, you're having Christmas with me and Grandma and Grandpa. Tomorrow you'll have Christmas with your dad. Just remember that both Dad and I love you, and that will always be the same."

Danny managed a wobbly smile.

"Fred Bear's feeling OK now," he said. "He's ready to eat."

"How about calling your dad first?" asked Danny's mom. "Would you like to do that?"

Danny nodded, and they hurried back into the warm house.

Dear Sally,

A lot's been going on around here. Mom and Dad had a big fight, and Dad moved out. Now they're getting a divorce. I hate it. I can't tell anyone at school – not even Emma. Her mom and dad are always hugging each other. She won't understand. What was it like when your dad left? I don't want to see my dad ever again. He calls every day, but I won't talk to him.

Mom is always snapping at me. She yells at me for being noisy. Then she yells at me for not talking to her.

School is ok. Our new teacher is Mrs. Roberts. She wears Doc Martens and smiles a lot. She asked me if anything was bothering me, and I said no.

Kate's having a sleepover next weekend, but I don't think I'll go. It's too much of a bother. Do you ever have sleepovers at your house?

Mom says I can come visit you sometime – if we can save up enough money.

Write soon.

Love,
Donna

Dear Donna,

It was great to hear from you!

You sound angry and fed up. That's just how I felt when my mom and dad split up. I wouldn't see my dad at first, either, but he kept coming over. At least talk to your dad on the phone, it will make you feel better. I bet he feels bad enough, without you ignoring him.

You say your Mom snaps at you. Grown-ups are weird. They want to split up, then, when they do, they still aren't happy. Maybe it takes them a while to get used to things. Maybe you should talk to your teacher about it and tell your friends. My friends here were great. Life might be rotten right now, but it'll be worse if you stay at home feeling crummy.

Things are better for me now. Dad visits once a week, and I stay at his place most weekends. We do crazy things together, like go fishing or string popcorn. My Mom's got a boyfriend. His name is Jasper!

Write soon.

Love,

Sally

P.S. Sure I have sleepovers! I invented them!

13

Feelings: It's Hard for Everyone

When you first hear that your parents are splitting up, it's natural to have all kinds of strong feelings.

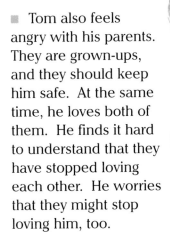

■ Tom feels sad that his family life has changed. He doesn't want his dad to live somewhere else. He wants things the way they used to be.

■ Tom also feels angry with his parents. They are grown-ups, and they should keep him safe. At the same time, he loves both of them. He finds it hard to understand that they have stopped loving each other. He worries that they might stop loving him, too.

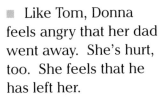

■ Like Tom, Donna feels angry that her dad went away. She's hurt, too. She feels that he has left her.

■ Donna doesn't want to tell her friends at school that her dad is gone. She feels that she's different from her friends now. She's worried about the future, too.

■ Children whose parents are getting a divorce are often bad-tempered and moody. Some find it hard to concentrate at school. Often, they are full of fears. Some of them feel that no one cares about them, and some worry about the parent who left home. Will they still get to see that parent?

■ It's a difficult time for parents, too. Some parents will be feeling like Tom's mom. She's sad that her marriage has ended, and she's worried about the future. She finds it hard, right now, to talk to Tom about his dad.

■ Tom's dad feels better since he left home. He couldn't

stand fighting anymore. At the same time, he's sad that he doesn't see Tom every day.

■ Tom's parents have different feelings and ideas, but they agree on one thing. They love Tom, and, no matter where they are living, they will always be his mom and dad.

■ When parents are worried and frightened themselves, it's often difficult for them to give you attention.

They might spend hours on the phone, talking things over with friends. They might snap at you for no reason, or burst into tears. They also might expect you to help out more at home.

■ If these changes seem cruel or unfair, tell someone. Talk to your mom or your dad. If you can't talk to them about it, talk to some other adult you trust.

15

How to Help Yourself Cope

When your parents are splitting up, you are bound to feel confused and sad. You might also feel hurt and angry. All these feelings are normal. You might even hate your mom and dad for what's happening, and that's OK, too. Sometimes, however, your feelings can be so strong that they are frightening. Here are some things you can do to help yourself cope:

- First of all, make sure you know what's going on. If there are any practical matters you're not sure about, such as where you'll sleep on weekends or who will be taking you to swimming lessons, then ask.

- Find someone to talk to about your feelings, fears, and worries. If your mom and dad are too upset to listen to you, tell an adult relative or friend, or even a teacher you like, about your feelings.

- Remember that your parents love you. They are not divorcing you, and nothing you said or did caused their separation.

- Remember, too, that you are not alone. There are many other children whose parents have split up, and who feel just like you.

- You don't have to take sides. It's important to stay in touch with both of your parents. Whether it's your mom or your dad who leaves home, you can call or write to the parent who left.

- If you feel that visiting arrangements get in the way of other things you want to do, such as football practice or drama club, speak up! Maybe the visiting schedule can be changed.

- Although you're sad, try to do the things you normally do. Keep up with your hobbies and activities and enjoy yourself with your friends.

Dear Grandma,

Mom said you had a cold and that a letter would cheer you up.

School vacation was great. I stayed four days with Dad and he took time off work. We painted my bedroom and put boats and ships on the wall. Dad did most of it but I helped. It's as good as my bedroom at home!

Dad's got a girlfriend. Her name's Linda. She came over for dinner but it felt funny because of my mom. She's not as pretty as Mom. She has a big nose. I don't know why my dad likes her. He doesn't need a girlfriend. He can come back home if he's lonely.

I hope you feel better soon.

When are you coming to see us again?

Love,

Tom

Dear Tom,

It was good to get a letter from you. My cold's almost gone now.

I'm glad that you and your dad enjoyed your time off of school. Your bedroom sounds super!

Try to be kind to Linda. If your dad likes her, I'm sure she's a nice person. Give her a chance and get to know her. You might make a new friend.

I know you'd really like your mom and dad to get together again, but that isn't going to happen, Tom, and you can't do anything about it. They are making new lives for themselves, and that means a new way of life for you.

We'll talk about it some more when I visit, if you want to. I'm coming in two weeks. I can't wait!

Love,
Grandma

19

Feelings: Better or Worse?

Even after your parents have been separated for a while, you might still feel sad and confused.

■ In time, your parents will probably start new relationships with other people. At first, Tom didn't like his dad's girlfriend. He felt guilty about being with her. He was worried that his mom would be upset. Thinking that Linda was supposed to replace his mom was painful for him.

■ Many parents decide to get married again or move in with someone new. At first, you might feel sad or angry, but you must finally stop hoping that your parents will get

■ Some children take a couple of years to settle into their new way of life. Other children worry when their parents seem to change — they might start wearing different clothes or trying new hobbies. Keep talking to them. Inside, they're still the same people they have always been.

back together. You might also find it hard to share your parents when you have been used to having them all to yourself. You might feel jealous and pushed aside, or you might not like their new partners.

■ All of these feelings are normal, and it's all right to talk about them. If you don't want to tell your mom or dad, find an adult relative or a teacher who will listen.

A Single-Parent Family

One or both of your parents might not have a new partner right away. You might then, like lots of other children, be part of what is called a single-parent family. You can still have fun with your friends, and you'll do things with your parent. Your parent will probably make some new friends who will also become part of your life.

Getting On with Your New Life

Some children get along well, from the very beginning, with their mom's and dad's new partners. For others, becoming part of a "stepfamily" might be more difficult. Sometimes there are new half-brothers and half-sisters to get along with, too. Here are some things that might help you get along better:

- Give everyone time. It takes a while to get to know new people. It might be two or three years before everyone in a stepfamily feels comfortable with each other. The right amount of time for you is however long it takes.

- No one expects you to love a new stepparent or stepfamily. Try to see them as friends. You can be friends with a stepparent and still love your real parent. Being friends with step-parents won't change your special feelings for your real parents.

- Each family has its own rules. Your real mom might not mind you jumping on the beds or eating in front of the television, but your stepmom might hate those things. Talk about the rules for each home and stick to them.

- Spend some time alone with each of your real parents. It's OK for you to ask them for this time.

- A stepfamily is a new situation for everyone, and everyone will make mistakes — even you. Try to give everyone a chance to adjust so the new situation will work out well.

- If you have any fears or worries about your new family, talk about them. Problems don't go away if you keep them a secret. If you can't talk to your mom or dad, talk to an adult relative or friend, or even a favorite teacher. Just be sure you choose an adult you trust.

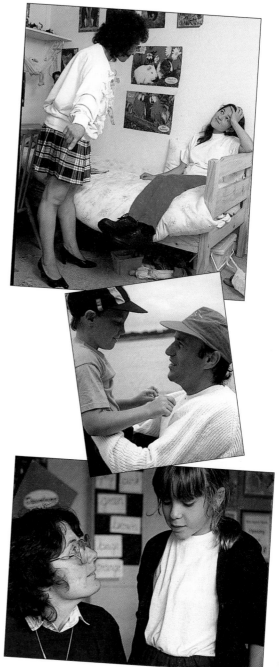

Locked Out

It was Friday afternoon. Kate and Gemma put on their coats and left school for the day. Gemma was going home. Kate was going to her dad's apartment.

Kate didn't say much. She kept her head down and dragged her feet. Gemma looked at her friend.

"I thought you liked it at your dad's place," she said.

"It used to be OK," replied Kate, sighing. "These days, Miss Perfect is always there."

Miss Perfect was Kate's dad's girlfriend. Her real name was Maria.

Gemma wrinkled her nose. She knew all about Maria's great clothes, important job, and fancy cooking. She was too good to be true, the girls had decided. They thought up the nickname together. But there was something Gemma didn't know. Miss Perfect and Kate's dad were getting married.

Kate waved goodbye to Gemma at the corner and walked on alone. It was starting to rain. As she walked, Kate imagined Maria in a long wedding dress, smiling a perfect smile. "Now Mom and Dad will never get back together," she thought sadly. She swallowed hard. Her throat felt sore.

At the apartment, Kate slowly climbed the steps and pressed the buzzer.

The door opened wide, and there stood Maria. She was dressed in black slacks and a shiny blouse.

"Come in!" she said.

"Where's Dad?" Kate asked quickly. He always got home from work early on Fridays.

"He's still in a meeting," explained Maria. She gave Kate a bright smile. "He'll be a little late today, I'm afraid."

Kate felt like she was going to burst into tears. She turned away before Maria could see and started back down the steps.

"Where are you going?" called Maria. "Come back!"

Suddenly, Kate felt angry.

"You can't tell me what to do. You're not my mom!" she shouted.

Kate marched along the pavement in the rain. She heard the apartment door slam and Maria's footsteps behind her.

"I've had just about enough," Maria panted, catching up. "I've rushed . . ."

Suddenly, Maria stopped. Kate turned around to look at her.

"We're locked out!" Maria groaned.

Kate waited to be scolded.

"Go on, put the blame on me," she told Maria, silently.

Instead, Maria began to laugh.

"What a perfect end to a rotten day!" she sputtered.

The rain was falling harder now. Maria looked up and down the street.

"What should we do?" she asked, shivering. "Your dad won't be back for quite a while."

"We could go to the café," Kate suggested.

"I don't have any money on me," Maria replied.

"I have some," said Kate.

Inside the café, Kate and Maria sat near a window with their drinks and stared out at the gray streets. At first, no one said anything. Kate thought about how young Maria looked with her hair all wet. She seemed much younger than Kate's mom. But Maria looked tired and cold, too, and Kate felt sorry for her.

The man at the next table was eating a hamburger, and it smelled really delicious.

"I'm starving," Maria whispered, rolling her eyes. "I had to work through lunch today."

Suddenly, Kate wanted to make everything all right. She dug into her school bag and pulled out all her loose change.

"I have enough money," she said proudly. "I can buy you a burger."

"OK," agreed Maria, "we'll split one!"

Munching her half of the burger, Kate watched Maria gobble up her share. She didn't look so perfect now. There was mustard on her cheek, and she had to keep blowing her nose. But she still seemed cheerful. "My mom would have a fit if I got her locked out in the rain," thought Kate.

"You've been really nice about all this," she told Maria, after a while.

"It was an accident," said Maria. She looked kindly at Kate. "I'm not trying to take your mom's place," she went on carefully, "but I'd like to be your friend."

Kate blushed. "OK," she said. And she realized that it really was OK.

Dear Sally,

Things have really changed for me. Remember I didn't see my dad for a while? Well, we finally started talking on the phone. Now I stay with him every two weeks, for the weekend. He moved to an old house in the country, and he has a dog named Jake. At Eastertime, we're going camping with Jake!

Mom and I are getting along really well, too. She has a part-time job so, sometimes, I go to Emma's house after school, and Mom picks me up there.

Mom and I are vegetarians now — just like you! Every week we try out a new recipe. It's fun. How is your family — and Jasper? (What a name!) Is he nice?

Write soon.

Love, Donna

Dear Donna,

Great to hear from you.

Guess what? Mom's getting married to Jasper. It's ok by me, he's a nice guy.

We had some trouble a while back. Jasper's kids came to stay for a week. They went in my room, they raided the refrigerator, and they used my felt pens without asking. We had a big fight. Then we all got together and talked it over. Jasper made us talk about it! He's great that way. And it worked! I guess I found it hard not to be the only kid anymore.

We're going camping, too. Jasper is going to take us to the mountains — to look for grizzlies! Are you afraid of bears?

Write soon.

Love, Sally

31

More Books to Read

■ *Families Are Forever! Kid's Workbook for sharing feelings about divorce.*
Melissa F. Smith
(Changing Lives Publications)

■ *Loon Summer.*
Barbara Santucci
(Wm. B. Eerdmans Publishing)

■ *On the Day His Daddy Left.*
Eric J. Adams and Kathleen Adams
(Albert Whitman & Co.)

■ *What Can I Do?: A Book for Children of Divorce.*
Danielle Lowry
(Magination Press)

Web Sites

■ Divorce Kids: A Child's Perspective.
www.divorce-kids.com

■ Kids' Turn: A non-profit organization to help kids and parents through divorce.
www.kidsturn.org